Secret Keeper Girl® Diary

Dannah Gresh

HARVEST House Publishers
EUGENE, OREGON

Cover and interior design by www.DesignbyJulia.com, Woodland Park, Colorado

Cover photo © Olga Kovalenko / Shutterstock

Interior photos by Steve Tressler / Mountainview Studios

Interior spot illustrations and doodle graphics by Julia Ryan and Shutterstock.com

SECRET KEEPER GIRL is a registered trademark of Dannah Gresh.

HARVEST KIDS is a registered trademark of The Hawkins Children's LLC. Harvest House Publishers, Inc., is the exclusive licensee of the federally registered trademark HARVEST KIDS.

MY SECRET KEEPER GIRL® DIARY

SKG!

Secret Keeper Girl Diary
A journal for all your best secrets!

Written by YOU!

Hi, Secret Keeper Girl!

I started keeping a diary or journal when I was about eight years old. It's a fun place to write down your secrets, thoughts, and memories.

But a journal can be so much more. It can be a place where you write down your prayers and things that God says to you. That's what it is for me. And I hope it will be for you.

This one has special Bible verses and quotes from all my favorite Secret Keeper Girl books. And keep an eye out for the fun fill-in spots that will get you thinking about all kinds of good stuff!

Enjoy!
Dannah Gresh

💚 My name is...

💚 One fun fact about me...

"...because you are precious to me. You are honored, and I love you."
(Isaiah 43:4b)

"You are a masterpiece created by God."

(Dannah Gresh)

"Your bodies are temples of the Holy Spirit, who is in you, whom you have received from God...You are not your own; you were bought at a price. Therefore honor God with your bodies."

(1 Corinthians 6:19-20 NIV)

My Secret Keeper Girl Diary!

"If I acted crazy,
I did it for God...
Christ's love has moved
me to such extremes.
His love has the first
and last word in
everything we do."

*(2 Corinthians 5:13,14 MSG:
Key verse from the Secret
Keeper Girl Crazy Hair Tour)*

my favorite thing to do when I'm not at school is...

"Always be joyful."

(1 Thessalonians 5:16)

DOODLE!
NOODLE!
DOODLE!

DOODLE!
NOODLE!
DOODLE!

"God could have made you and me from the dust of the ground. He proved it by creating Adam. But he chose to make females 'out of' man. This way we know God's intentions for sure. We are not two separate species battling it out for who is the best or the strongest or God's favorite. We are one."

(Suzy Weibel, A Girl's Guide to Understanding Boys)

"True love was God's idea! He designed marriage love to be a lasting, ride-into-the-sunset kind of love. He himself said, 'Love never fails.'"

(1 Corinthians 13:8 NASB: Bob Gresh, 8 Great Dates for Dads and Daughters: Talking to Your Daughter About Understanding Boys)

💗 my favorite love story in the Bible is...

My Secret Keeper Girl Diary!

"Your beauty should not come from outward adornment, such as elaborate hairstyles and the wearing of gold jewelry or fine clothes. Rather, it should be that of your inner self, the unfading beauty of a gentle and quiet spirit, which is of great worth in God's sight."

(1 Peter 3:3-4 NIV)

"Do everything without grumbling or arguing, so that you may become blameless and pure, 'children of God without fault in a warped and crooked generation.' Then you will shine among them like stars in the sky."

(Philippians 2:14-15 NIV)

💟 My mom's name:

💟 My dad's name:

💟 Things I like to do with my parents:

"Honor your father and mother, so that you may live long in the land."

(Exodus 20:12 NIV)

My Secret Keeper Girl Diary!

DOODlE!
NOODlE!
DOODlE!

DOODLE!
NOODLE!
DOODLE!

A woman of God
"is clothed with strength
and dignity."

(Proverbs 31:25)

❤ Three special things about
my grandma and grandpa:

1.

2.

3.

"Clothes aren't the only things we wear. God invites us to 'wear' things on the inside too. [You need to] discover some of the hottest fashion for the heart."

(Dannah Gresh, 8 Great Dates for Moms and Daughters)

"God is tickled silly pink madly in love with you."

(Jonathan and Suzy Weibel, from the Secret Keeper Girl Pajama Party Tour)

"Real physical beauty is those special things about you that are unlike anyone else. Kind of funny, isn't it? Those are sometimes the things that make us feel most uncomfortable because they're...well, different. But God says that's what makes us beautiful."

(Dannah Gresh, 8 Great Dates for Moms and Daughters*)*

"My dove, my
perfect one,
is unique."

(Song of Songs 6:9 NIV)

❤ Here are the names of my friends:

❤ Things we like to do together:

"**Friends** are supposed to make us better people."

(Dannah Gresh, A Girl's Guide to Best Friends and Mean Girls)

"Humility is the invitation Jesus makes to you and me. We don't get to be waited on hand and foot, envied, or pampered. We get to serve."

(*Dannah Gresh,* A Girl's Guide to Best Friends and Mean Girls)

My Secret Keeper Girl Diary!

"What if instead of chasing after what is normal, we choose to be girls who chase after what is special? Or we could even say, Why don't we become girls who chase after what is crazy? Let's be different!"

(Suzy Weibel, A Girl's Guide to Understanding Boys*)*

If I had a whole day to spend with my best friend, we would...

"Friends not only reflect who we are, but they also say a lot about who we are becoming."

(Dannah Gresh, A Girl's Guide to Best Friends and Mean Girls*)*

"The king of kings
has chosen *you* as a friend!"

*(Dannah Gresh, A Girl's Guide
to Best Friends and Mean
Girls)*

DOODLE!
NOODLE!
DOODLE!

DOODLE!
NOODLE!
DOODLE!

"Being like Jesus means more than forgiving. It means bringing our friends close to us again by loving on them. It's hard to love on someone who has hurt us. And no one knows that better than your best friend, Jesus."

(Dannah Gresh, A Girl's Guide to Best Friends and Mean Girls*)*

My Secret Keeper Girl Diary!

"Jesus talks about you!
He wants to. It freely flows
out of his mouth. He is totally
telling all the angels and God
the Father about you!"

(Dannah Gresh, A Girl's Guide to
Best Friends and Mean Girls*)*

Three things that are great about Jesus...

1.

2.

3.

"If we speak out
freely for God,
then he will speak out
freely for us!"

(Dannah Gresh, A Girl's
Guide to Best Friends and
Mean Girls*)*

"To live in God's constant protection and provision depends at least in part on how much we live for him."

(Dannah Gresh, A Girl's Guide to Best Friends and Mean Girls)

"Jesus calls us friends, and his word is a blueprint for how to be just like him. So there you have it—the Bible is one of the world's premier textbooks on how to be a friend!"

(Dannah Gresh, A Girl's Guide to Best Friends and Mean Girls)

"The most famous person ever to walk the face of this earth loves me and wants to be my friend."

(Dannah Gresh, A Girl's Guide to Best Friends and Mean Girls*)*

❥ my school...

❥ my teachers...

❥ my favorite subjects...
and why I like them so much!

"love, joy, peace, patience, kindness, gentleness, faithfulness, goodness, self-control...these are the words that begin to define us when we make it a habit to obey."

(Dannah Gresh, A Girl's Guide to Best Friends and Mean Girls*)*

My Secret Keeper Girl Diary!

DOODLE!
NOODLE!
DOODLE!

DOODLE!
NOODLE!
DOODLE!

"Friendship with Jesus is such a good thing we simply cannot keep it to ourselves."

(Dannah Gresh, A Girl's Guide to Best Friends and Mean Girls)

Dear Jesus, thank you for being my friend!
I want you to know...

"Jesus never stops
thinking about you
or talking to God about
you on your behalf."

(Dannah Gresh, A Girl's Guide
to Best Friends and Mean Girls*)*

"When Jesus said, 'I chose you' to his friends, he meant these words for you and me too. So get this...Jesus picks you. Every time. Every day. He picks you, girl!"

(Dannah Gresh, A Girl's Guide to Best Friends and Mean Girls*)*

"Real physical beauty is those special things about you that are unlike anyone else."

(Dannah Gresh, 8 Great Dates for Moms and Daughters*)*

"Don't forget that God wants to comfort you."

(Dannah Gresh, 8 Great Dates for Moms and Daughters*)*

❤ Dear God, sometimes I worry about...

"God created you with an intoxicating power called *beauty*. It's your responsibility to handle it with care."

(Dannah Gresh, 8 Great Dates for Moms and Daughters)

My Secret Keeper Girl Diary!

"God wants you to look like a girl who worships him. Since worshipping him fills us with joy, we need to make sure we don't clothe ourselves in dark and dreary attire."

(Dannah Gresh, 8 Great Dates for Moms and Daughters*)*

"The source of true beauty is the presence of God!"

(Dannah Gresh, 8 Great Dates for Moms and Daughters*)*

Three things that are unique or special about me:

1.

2.

3.

DOODLE!
NOODLE!
DOODLE!

DOODLE!
NOODLE!
DOODLE!

"Your value comes from God. Not from anyone or anything else. He made you to be unique—one of a kind."

(Bob Gresh, 8 Great Dates for Dads and Daughters: Talking to Your Daughter About Understanding Boys*)*

"God is knocking at
the door of your life."

(Dannah Gresh, 8 Great Dates
for Moms and Daughters)

💕 If I could spend a day doing
all the things I like, I would...

"My diary is filled with days where the first thought I recorded was, 'Today was so boring!' Here's a little something for you scientifically minded girls—the 24 hours we call a day are 'values-neutral.' This means they are neither good nor bad. They are not exciting or boring. They are only what we make of them. A day cannot be boring. But we, as human beings, can be bored. The choice is up to us."

(Suzy Weibel, A Girl's Guide to Understanding Boys)

"He loves you, and he knows that when you spend time alone with him it gives you confidence, helps you to know your value in Christ, steers you in the right direction, and gives you internal beauty."

(Dannah Gresh, 8 Great Dates for Moms and Daughters)

"Do you spend more time in front of the mirror making yourself externally beautiful, or do you spend more time developing your inner beauty through quiet communion with God?"

(Dannah Gresh, 8 Great Dates for Moms and Daughters*)*

I get most excited when I'm getting ready to go...

"You can believe in something if it is true. When there's someone in your life you can always believe, it is easy to trust them."

(Dannah Gresh, A Girl's Guide to Best Friends and Mean Girls*)*

"It's okay to want something because you think it's neat, but watch out when you start buying things just because your friends have them."

(Dannah Gresh, 8 Great Dates for Moms and Daughters*)*

♥ my favorites!

Book:

Movie:

Song:

Pet:

TV show:

Sport:

Color:

Ice-cream flavor:

"We show our love
to God through trust
and obedience."

(Dannah Gresh, A Girl's Guide
to Best Friends and Mean
Girls*)*

My Secret Keeper Girl Diary!

DOODLE!
NOODLE!
DOODLE!

DOODLE!
NOODLE!
DOODLE!

"The friendship of God is like no other relationship. We need to enjoy him and laugh with him—we need to worship and honor him with all that we are."

(Dannah Gresh, A Girl's Guide to Best Friends and Mean Girls*)*

"The Bible doesn't ignore beauty.
It does, however, say over and over again that when we define beauty by what is on the outside, we make a huge mistake!"

(Dannah Gresh, A Girl's Guide to Best Friends and Mean Girls*)*

♥ My birthday!
The three best things about a birthday:

1.

2.

3.

"God doesn't just dance over us when we do something great or worthy of praise. He dances over us just because we are near."

(Dannah Gresh, A Girl's Guide to Best Friends and Mean Girls*)*

My Secret Keeper Girl Diary!

"If you keep my commands,
you will remain in my love, just as I
have kept my Father's commands
and remain in his love."

(John 15:10 NIV)

"God is willing to go to extreme measures to express his joy over you!"

(Dannah Gresh, A Girl's Guide to Best Friends and Mean Girls*)*

"The best remedy I've found for overcoming jealousy is to do everything I can to control my focus. Our focus shouldn't be on other people. It should be on God. As we learn more about him, we'll become truly thrilled with who he created us to be."

(Dannah Gresh, A Girl's Guide to Best Friends and Mean Girls*)*

Dear God, today this is what's on my heart...

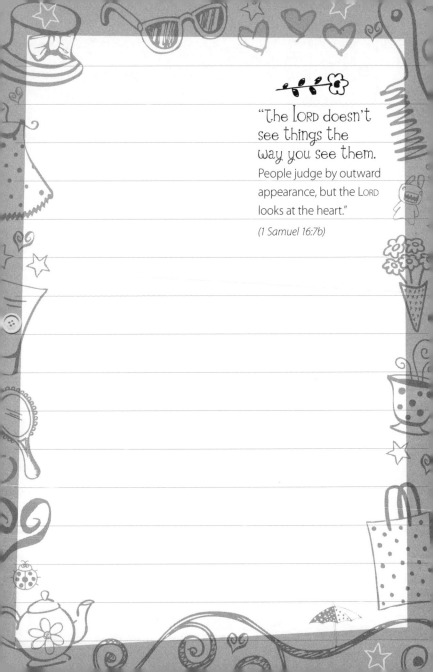

"The LORD doesn't see things the way you see them. People judge by outward appearance, but the LORD looks at the heart."

(1 Samuel 16:7b)

"A lot of times, jealousy is all about focusing on what we're *not* rather than what we are!"

(Dannah Gresh, A Girl's Guide to Best Friends and Mean Girls)

DOODlE!
nOODlE!
DOODlE!

DOODLE!
NOODLE!
DOODLE!

"Today is a chance
to get better.
Today is a chance to
get stronger in your best
race. Today is one step
closer to your lifelong
dream."

(Suzy Weibel, A Girl's Guide
to Understanding Boys*)*

My Secret Keeper Girl Diary!

"When we know someone, it creates the knowledge we need to have hope for them."

(Dannah Gresh, A Girl's Guide to Best Friends and Mean Girls*)*

Five nice things I can do for a friend...

1.

2.

3.

4.

5.

"If you are pursuing true love, you'll find yourself willing to go out and do extraordinary acts of kindness for people you don't even know."

(Dannah Gresh, A Girl's Guide to Best Friends and Mean Girls*)*

"You, LORD, are our Father. We are the clay, you are the potter; we are all the work of your hand."

(Isaiah 64:8 NIV)

"Real love hopes."

(Dannah Gresh, A Girl's Guide to Best Friends and Mean Girls*)*

"You're blessed when you get your inside world—your mind and heart—put right. Then you can see God in the outside world."

(Matthew 5:8 MSG)

"God created us to desire unfailing love."

(Dannah Gresh, A Girl's Guide to Best Friends and Mean Girls)

❤ Three things I love, love, love...and why!

I.

2.

3.

"It takes us most of our lives to learn the fact that there's only one Source we can plug into and find unfailing love: God."

(Dannah Gresh, A Girl's Guide to Best Friends and Mean Girls)

"I praise you, for I am fearfully and wonderfully made. Wonderful are your works; my soul knows it very well."

(Psalm 139:14 ESV)

"A true friend is one who chooses friendship over popularity, money, or image."

(Dannah Gresh, A Girl's Guide to Best Friends and Mean Girls)

"We are God's masterpiece. He has created us anew in Christ Jesus, so we can do the good things he planned for us long ago."

(Ephesians 2:10)

My Secret Keeper Girl Diary!

DOODLE!
NOODLE!
DOODLE!

DOODLE!
NOODLE!
DOODLE!

When I grow up, I'd like to...

"Hope: the feeling that what is wanted can be had."

(Dannah Gresh, A Girl's Guide to Best Friends and Mean Girls*)*

"The heartfelt counsel of a friend is as sweet as perfume and incense."

(Proverbs 27:9)

"He comforts
us in all our
troubles so that
we can comfort
others. When they
are troubled, we will
be able to give them
the same comfort
God has given us."

(2 Corinthians 1:4)

♥ Three ways I've helped a friend feel better:

1.

2.

3.

> "When you truly love God, you obey him."

(Dannah Gresh, Secret Keeper: The Delicate Power of Modesty)

"God's Word says that everything he has created is *good*. He made you! You are therefore *good*! The fact that he made you *is your worth*! Period!

(Secret Keeper Girl Crazy Hair Tour)

"In God's eyes,
you are beautiful.
In the eyes of the
one who made you,
you are *treasured*!"

*(Secret Keeper Girl
Crazy Hair Tour)*

God, I'm happy you love me!

Here's what I can do today because I love you...

"Even now God expects you to stand out and live and act differently. He created you to do just that. You might even look a little...*crazy!*"

(Secret Keeper Girl Crazy Hair Tour)

My Secret Keeper Girl Diary!

"Put on every piece of God's armor so you will be able to resist the enemy in the time of evil. Then after the battle you will still be standing firm. Stand your ground, putting on the belt of truth and the body armor of God's righteousness. For shoes, put on the peace that comes from the Good News so that you will be fully prepared. In addition to all of these, hold up the shield of faith to stop the fiery arrows of the devil. Put on salvation as your helmet, and take the sword of the Spirit, which is the word of God."

(Ephesians 6:13-17)

DOODLE!
NOODLE!
DOODLE!

DOODLE!
NOODLE!
DOODLE!

"Our God is not normal. He loves like *crazy*!"

(Secret Keeper Girl Crazy Hair Tour)

"Obviously, I'm not trying to win the approval of people, but of God. If pleasing people were my goal, I would not be Christ's servant."

(Galatians 1:10)

This is the craziest thing I've ever done...

"normal is overrated."

(Secret Keeper Girl Crazy Hair Tour)

"She is clothed with strength and dignity, and she laughs without fear of the future."

(Proverbs 31:25)

"A friend loves
at all times."

(Proverbs 17:17a NIV)

"This truth gives them confidence that they have eternal life, which God—who does not lie—promised them before the world began."

(Titus 1:2)

"A man of many companions may come to ruin, but there is a friend who sticks closer than a brother."

(Proverbs 18:24 ESV)

My Secret Keeper Girl Diary!

"Pursue love."

(1 Corinthians 14:1a ESV)

❤ Three ways I can show
mom and Dad I love them...

1.

2.

3.

"This is my commandment, that you love one another as I have loved you. Greater love has no one than this, that someone lay down his life for his friends. You are my friends if you do what I command you."

(John 15:12-14 ESV)

"The LORD your God is with you, the Mighty Warrior who saves. He will take great delight in you; in his love he will no longer rebuke you, but will rejoice over you with singing."

(Zephaniah 3:17 NIV)

"Women who claim to be devoted to God should make themselves attractive by the good things they do."

(1 Timothy 2:10)

"His unfailing love toward those who fear him is as great as the height of the heavens above the earth. He has removed our sins as far from us as the east is from the west."

(Psalm 103:11-12)

DOODLE!
NOODLE!
DOODLE!

DOODLE!
NOODLE!
DOODLE!

"Let the king be
enthralled by
your beauty...
All glorious is the
princess within her
chamber."

(Psalm 45:11,13 NIV)

♥ My five favorite things about my room:

1.

2.

3.

4.

5.

"The wages of sin is death, but the free gift of God is eternal life in Christ Jesus our Lord."

(Romans 6:23 ESV)

"Trust steadily in God, hope unswervingly, love extravagantly. And the best of the three is love."

(1 Corinthians 13:13b MSG)

My Secret Keeper Girl Diary!

"Those who look to him
are radiant; their faces are
never covered with shame."

(Psalm 34:5 NIV)

Thank you, God, for...

SECRET KEEPER GIRL® SERIES

A Girl's Guide to Best Friends and Mean Girls

Dannah Gresh and Suzy Weibel

If you're a girl, buckle up for some friendship drama. Some things about friendships are great, like BFFs—and some things are really hard, like dealing with mean girls!

In *A Girl's Guide to Best Friends and Mean Girls*, we help you rewrite the script to experience friendship with Jesus as your role model. Quizzes, puzzles, meditations, and biblical advice will help you get closer to him, your truly best friend. And as you do, you'll get better at being friends with everyone! You'll find answers to questions like these:

- Who should I choose for friends?
- What do I do about jealousy and hurts in my friendships? How about mean girls?
- How can I be Jesus' friend, and how do I introduce others to him?

A Girl's Guide to Best Friends and Mean Girls gives you everything you need to build better friendships.

SECRET KEEPER GIRL® SERIES

A Girl's Guide to Understanding Boys

Dannah Gresh and Suzy Weibel

Everyone—including your aunt who constantly asks, "Do you have a boyfriend yet?"—seems to think that being boy-crazy is normal. Dannah Gresh and Suzy Weibel think that *normal* is overrated! What if instead of chasing after what is normal, you get God-crazy instead and follow his advice when it comes to boys?

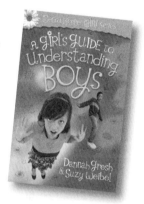

A Girl's Guide to Understanding Boys will help you do just that. It's full of quizzes, puzzles, meditations, and biblical advice on how to deal with the boy stuff that's going to come into your life sooner or later. Connect with answers to questions like...

- Why are all my friends boy-crazy? Should *I* be?
- Who do I listen to about handling relationships with guys?
- How can I stand out from the crowd and pursue purity without losing my friends?
- What should my parents have to do with my future dating life?

Half the people in the world are boys. Here's a great start to understanding them in the best way!

And for you and your mom...

8 GREAT DATES
Talking with Your Daughter About Best Friends and Mean Girls

Dannah Gresh

One of the best ways to guide your girl toward healthy friendships is to spend quality time with her yourself. The popular 8 Great Dates series from Secret Keeper Girl offers the most fun you'll ever have digging into God's Word with your daughter. (Think: shopping sprees, slumber parties, ding-dong-ditching, and more!) Eight creative dates help you and your daughter tackle questions like…

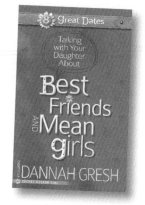

- Why do I feel jealous of my BFF sometimes?
- How should I act when I get left out?
- Is it okay to be boy-crazy?

Creative ideas and godly guidance help you bond with your daughter and protect her as she navigates the crazy tween world of friendships using God's truth as her standard.

For you and your dad...

8 GREAT DATES FOR DADS AND DAUGHTERS
Talking with Your Daughter About Understanding Boys

Bob Gresh and Dannah Gresh

Our culture pressures girls to crush on boys way too soon. A dad's involvement in his daughter's growing interest is the greatest protection against her getting her heart broken by moving too fast.

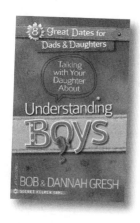

These *8 Great Dates* help a father and his 8- to 12-year-old daughter connect on topics that really matter. But don't expect this to be boring Sunday-school talk. This is fun stuff! (Think: pulling pranks, stargazing, treasure hunting, and more as you consider God's Word together!)

You'll tackle big questions from your daughter's point of view...

- What was God thinking when he created girls to like boys?
- Why is everyone boy-crazy? Should *I* be?
- When can I start to date? (It's not too soon to talk about it!)
- How can I embrace purity?

A personal pullout section for your daughter and online audio conversations with Bob and Dannah offer more ways to build your connection—and to love and protect your little girl as she grows up.

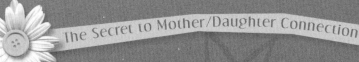

The Secret to Mother/Daughter Connection

What is a
Secret Keeper Girl?

Well, she's a lot of things. And she's NOT a lot of things. She's NOT a mean girl. She's a girl whose friendships are full of kindness. She's NOT boy crazy. (Moms, can we get an Amen?) She's a girl who knows she can share all of her heart-secrets with her mom at any time.

She's also a girl who embraces modesty. Why? Because she knows that she is a masterpiece created by God. She strives to keep the deepest secrets of her authentic beauty a secret! Maybe you are new to our movement, or maybe you are a long-time Secret Keeper Girl who has been to a live event. Maybe you have already read "Secret Keeper" and been on eight great dates with your Momma! Regardless, you, sweet girl, are a Secret Keeper Girl because you are a masterpiece created by God's hand.

Secret Keeper GIRL

SecretKeeperGirl.com

Like us on Facebook!
Follow us on Twitter!